Robert F. (Robert Forman) Horton

The conquered world : and other papers

Robert F. (Robert Forman) Horton

The conquered world : and other papers

ISBN/EAN: 9783741176449

Manufactured in Europe, USA, Canada, Australia, Japa

Cover: Foto ©Andreas Hilbeck / pixelio.de

Manufactured and distributed by brebook publishing software (www.brebook.com)

Robert F. (Robert Forman) Horton

The conquered world : and other papers

ANDOVER-HARVARD THEOLOGICAL
LIBRARY

MDCCCCX

CAMBRIDGE, MASSACHUSETTS

THE CONQUERED WORLD,
And Other Papers.

By R. F. Horton, M.A., D.D.

LONDON: JAMES CLARKE & CO.,
13 & 14, Fleet Street. 1898.

First Edition, April, 1898.

ANDOVER-HARVARD
THEOLOGICAL LIBRARY
CAMBRIDGE, MASS.

Contents.

	PAGE
The Conquered World	1
Desidia and Alacritas	24
The Garden of Lilies	38
A Call to Work	60
The Meaning of Spring	73
On Getting Out of Ruts	84
Dawn	103
R. L. Stevenson's Christmas Sermon	116

The Conquered World.

"Be of good cheer; I have overcome the world."—JOHN XVI. 33.

IT is the parting message which the Lord gave to His disciples as a body. After that He turned to pray to the Father for them, and then spoke no more with them. The words were therefore designed, no doubt, to ring out as the keynote of the Christian's life and of the Church's history until He comes. Set this side by side with the parting message of Buddha. He, as He was dying, said to His disciples, "Work out your salvation with diligence." This is a noble, a necessary, we might even say, a Christian precept. But it presents a remarkable contrast, as the farewell utterance of a religious leader, with the words of Jesus which are now in our ears. The one message suggests travail and effort; the other suggests victory. The words of Buddha throw men on their own resources; the words of Christ throw them on the strength of Another. This message breathes despondency; that breathes hope. The contrast will almost explain why it is that wherever Buddha is saviour pessimism, and wherever Christ is Saviour optimism, prevails.

Yet there are some Christians whose general tone and practice seem to imply that they are more familiar with Buddha's last words than with Christ's. "Work out your own salvation with diligence" has been the keynote of many strenuous, well-meant Christian lives. But when Christianity has been triumphant and progressive it has been so in virtue of these thrilling words of its Leader. It has failed, and it does fail, whenever Christian men forget them, or lose their meaning, or do not appropriate them in such a way as to connect themselves with the force of which they speak.

It was a remark of Mr. Ruskin's that the Christian Pulpit fails in its effect because it speaks so much of what men must do to earn salvation, and so little of what God has done to give it. To dwell too strenuously on the things we have to do fosters the Buddhist tendency in us all, and harmonises only too well with the claim to personal merit which we are always disposed to make. On the other hand, it requires much grace and humility to be always insisting on the transcendent facts of the Christian Redemption, which exclude boasting, and place all, even the best of us, in the lowly attitude of recipients.

Now let us try to see what the Lord meant by this last message of His; and if the meaning should dawn upon our minds while we are considering it, we may encourage one another to accept the truth, and then to live in the spirit of this creed. It may, perhaps, surprise us to find that we have attached very little definite meaning to the words. Like many other of His thoughts which have become the commonplaces of Christianity, this is not much observed. For we do not stop to geologise on the flagstones of the pavement, and the familiar truths of the Gospel often pass almost as unnoticed and unexplored. It is quite conceivable that many truly Christian people have never faced the full force of the words. Let me repeat them, marking by an emphasis the implied contrast: "These things I have spoken to you, that *in Me* ye may have peace; *in the world* you have tribulation, but be of good courage, *I* have overcome *the world.*"

This is the language of a conqueror. Two forces had been engaged, the world and Jesus. Jesus had gained the victory. We, presumably all of us, are either *in the world* or *in Jesus*. If we are in the world we stand on defeated ground, and are exposed to all the penalties of defeat. If we are in Jesus we stand upon the Conqueror's ground, and share the fruits of His victory; we have the peace which His prowess has won.

We will concentrate our thought

for a moment on the words: "I have conquered the world." It is possible, and easy, to give them two meanings, one of which would make the statement untrue, the other of which would deprive it of practical power. We might take them to mean either "I have already subdued the whole world to Myself, and won all mankind to My allegiance"—this would be untrue—or, "I have obtained a personal victory over the worldly powers"—this would be ineffectual.

The first of these meanings is quite out of the question, for "we see not yet all things subjected to Him." To many it seems quite the contrary. There is a general impression—even among Christian men—that the victory of Christ is, to say the least of it, very imperfect. Many in their hearts think that the conflict between Christ and the world ended really in favour of the world. It slew Him. It has perverted His teaching. It has travestied His thought. It has resisted His Church, and when resistance has seemed giving way, it has subtlely stolen within the entrenchments, and as a traitor has betrayed the position to the foe. There are Christians who are too sad to say much about it; they try not to think of it; but it is their shuddering conviction that the world has proved too much for their Lord. They see Him in their imagination, as Clough saw Him, a pale, discomfited Ghost that sits upon that far-off tomb "by the lorn Syrian town." This we may hold to be exaggerated, and deficient in spiritual insight; but that it is possible for honest men to take such a view shows that we cannot understand the words in the way proposed, for that would make them an idle boast.

But the second meaning is open to objections almost as serious. Suppose He only meant that He had obtained a personal victory over the world by resisting its temptations, and turning aside from its attractions in the way which is described in the Gospels. That He did obtain such a victory, few will be prepared to deny. But so, in a certain sense, did Buddha. There are even points in the renunciation made by the Hindu prince, and in the story of his self-sacrificing life, which make one wonder whether in that personal sense he did not as truly vanquish the world as Christ did. Indeed, there have been many examples of such a victory. And it is not necessary to underrate the influence which these examples exercise over us all. To know that there has been even One who has been proof against the world, unseduced by its allurements, undazzled by its splendours, unaffrighted by its terrors, is a strength and a joy to all earnest souls that pay attention to the fact. And merely from this point of view the unworldly life of Jesus, passed in the world, affords a rallying-point for noble effort, and exercises a constant power over the thoughts of men. But how inadequate would this be to account for the inspiriting words, "Be of good cheer." Nay, if we are to suppose that this is all He meant by overcoming the world, the exhortation is not wholly free from a tone of mockery. "In the world you have tribulation, you are exposed to its perpetual trials, and borne down by its terrific onsets; but, courage, I have escaped it, I have been superior to it. You are defeated in the fray; but see, I sit on the hill above the tumult—beyond the reach of harm." It is a thought of despair. What can it profit you, when you are carried away by the vain ambitions of the world, tormented by its inworking lusts, or overwhelmed by its accumulated sorrows, to be told that He, the strong One, overcame; that He scorned the repute of men, the wealth, the comfort which might have been within His reach, that He showed no weak point to the assaults of sensual passion, that in acute pain or heartbreaking sorrow He could say, "I have overcome"?

I have dwelt upon these two obvious meanings—I might almost

say natural meanings — of the words, because, perhaps, some of us are tempted to abide in them, and so to miss the real meaning. If, therefore, you have been in the habit of attaching one or other of these interpretations to the last message of Christ, will you admit the force of what has just been said, and recognise that you have not yet arrived at what is really meant?

Brood upon the words, let them tell their own tale, and you will presently see that they could mean nothing less than this: *The World*, in the familiar sense of the term, which it would be a needless diversion to define, was too much for man; it mastered him and held him in bondage. Like a strong man armed it kept the house in which we were obliged to live, with a kind of brute right over us. Just as before 1862 the negroes of the United States were born into slavery, so men were born into the house of bondage, sold under sin. It is difficult to conceive what this malignant Power was in its pristine force, for we only see it now in a manner vanquished. Yet, broken and unmasked, how strong it still is, and what an incredible fascination it exercises over us as men! But Jesus engaged in a hand to hand conflict with this Power. His earthly life from beginning to end was a tussle of this kind. In the main it was waged in the Invisible; but from time to time signs appeared, and those who were about Him saw the agitation on His face and were amazed, saw the sweat as great drops of blood, heard the agonised cry as of a soul forsaken by God. But that conflict, difficult for us to conceive, because the Power against which He strove is to us intangible and almost inconceivable, ended in His victory. He entered the house of the strong man armed, and spoiled him; He took captivity captive; he broke the sceptre, and overturned the throne. Just as the proclamation of slave-emancipation in America made every slave free who chose to claim his freedom, so the victory of Jesus secured a complete victory for all men who would enter into it. He could say, at the last, with a clear confidence, that the fight was finished, "I have conquered the world," and then He ascended up on high, leading captivity captive, to receive gifts for men.

Henceforth no man need be enslaved to the world. Freedom was purchased for all. And when

He gathered His chosen disciples about Him to send them out as messengers He did not tell them to proclaim "work out your salvation with diligence; wrestle, fight, and overcome." But He charged them to proclaim the glad and significant tidings, that He had overcome, victory was secured, and whoever would believe might enter into the fruits of it, and into that peace which is the desired result of victory.

Here we are touching on words which are very familiar, too familiar almost to retain our attention. But this is the very point where men frequently miss the whole bearing of the situation. They see and admit in a vague way that Christ obtained such a victory as has been described, but they make no further use of the fact. *They do not see how to appropriate it.* And, consequently, with this great fact before them, and with His thought of love ever pressing upon them, they turn aside to wage their own warfare, to strive for their own victory. Instead of standing on victorious ground and sharing a victory that is gained, they continue to think that they have to gain the victory themselves, and enter on a course of Christian life which is—how can it be otherwise?—an unbroken series of defeats.

We have not to gain a victory, but to enter on a victory gained.

Let me attempt an illustration. I remember reading an account, I think it was, of the Eiffel Tower in a thunderstorm. There was an aerial chamber in which one might sit, with the lightnings a-play on every side. Indeed, the lofty summit attracted the electric currents, and drew them to the ground. But the chamber was so constructed that one within it remained unscathed. In the centre of commotion, circled by the electric blaze, there where all the storm was raging, he was safer than in the most sheltered retreat. Christ's victory means that here, right in the midst of this tumultuous and perilous world, He has secured an impenetrable refuge, the enchanted chamber of victory. It is entered by faith, and there one may smile at the impotent rage of the world. Unscathed, unalarmed, in Him and Him alone we may be secure.

But if this image conveys a true idea, it must evidently make all the difference conceivable, whether we take our stand in the charmed chamber of victory or outside it. A Christian who is just outside it may be exposed to greater peril than a person who is far away from it. He is in the centre of the conflict; but he has no victory except his own to rely on, and that victory is very uncertain.

Now, can we help one another to a practical conclusion? For the great difference between Christians is not one of creed or church, but rather this practical difference, that some Christians have found the way of sharing Christ's victory, while others are seeking to gain a victory of their own, almost as if His victory had been a mere chimera.

Place side by side the Master's utterance, and that of His beloved disciple: "Be of good cheer, I have overcome the world," said the Master. "This is the victory that overcometh the world, even your faith," said the disciple.

Christ's is a victory achieved once for all; ours is merely the appropriation of His by faith. Put it in this way. When you genuinely believe in Christ, and look at things from the standpoint of His cross, you see the world as a vanquished power, the fetters of sin broken, the glamour of its lusts dissipated. You see the principalities and powers led in captivity as Jesus "makes a show of them openly." Within the circle of His victory the world's promises seem idle, its pleasures pains, its successes perils, just as, within the circle of the world, the spiritual things appear unreal, and the voice of Jesus sounds faint and distant. It is by faith that you step within the circle of His victory and occupy that point of outlook for life and time. By faith you take your place within the lines of

His accomplished work, so that the spell of the world is broken, its pomp exposed as a vain show, its unreality demonstrated to perception.

The words seem cold and inadequate to convey the thought to one who is not disposed to make the personal experiment. But let us push into detail, to give such concrete and tangible reality to the subject as it admits of in speech.

Christ has vanquished sin. But you are assailed by some too familiar sin. It has overcome you before, and it threatens to do so again. Like swelling tides, it rises to submerge the soul, and you do not see how you can take arms against it. It has effected some entrance within. You strive, but it seems in vain. You pray, but prayer seems useless. Now take that step of faith, which sets you in the circle of Christ's victory. Recognise that He has overcome; that this very sin is what He has overcome; that it is a monster whose power is broken. Now what happens? The effect is miraculous. Those swelling floods subside. From the face of witchery the mask is torn, and the hideous lineaments appear. Passion dies. The soul is borne up on a strength not its own. The invisible stream of power—Christ's victory—sets easily against the combined forces of sin. No words can explain the sweetness and joy of that experience.

But the world is with us not only as an allurement to personal sin. It often presents its most depressing front to us as a combination of evils with which we have no power to cope. Often, as just now, the grim monsters of reaction, of corruption, of materialism, of sensuality, of superstition and its companion doubt, surge up against the feeble defences of the Church, bearing down the unarmed protectors of her walls.

Who can take arms against this sea of evils? Now, it is precisely in this broader issue of the world's sin and ruin, that, if we would be but advised, we should more eagerly still take refuge by faith in the achieved victory of our Lord. Not only can this alone bring us assurance and peace; this alone can still the angry tumult and bring calm after storm.

When I was crossing the Atlantic in the *Umbria*, I was told how on the previous voyage the main shaft of the propellor had snapped, and the great ship lay helpless at the mercy of the seas.

A gale was blowing, and with such force that soon there was serious apprehension, as the vast waves broke over the upper decks with terrific force, and there was no steering "way" to put the prow to the seas. And then when the uneasiness was at its height, the captain had some barrels of oil poured out of the portholes.

What a trifling thing it seemed; how impossible to calm those raging waters, and to provide a safe riding for that enormous hulk by such a simple operation! But presently the waves were calmed, none broke on deck, and the ship rode easily on the waters.

This simple step by faith into the victory of Christ produces a a similar effect. It not only calms the troubled spirit and gives peace within, it actually stills the waters. That is to say, there is no other way of successfully opposing the forces of evil, of taking the Gospel to the heathen, or of bringing our own country into the enjoyment of it, but by fearlessly stepping out on the fact that Christ has overcome.

We are trying to do too much. We are not giving play to the great thing that is done. We fight bravely a losing battle, instead of standing boldly in the battle won.

There are many who are waking up to this truth, and miracles are wrought by their hands; they in their turn wake us; but as the hosts of the Lord become generally and habitually alive to it, the reality of Christ's victory will appear in all its magnitude, and we shall march, each man straight before him, over the prostrate walls to take possession, in His name, of the conquered world.

Desidia and Alacritas.

Romans xiii. 11-14.

It is a merciful arrangement that we live by *days*, and are able to begin afresh every twenty-four hours. It is merciful in itself, for sleep "knits up the ravelled sleeve of care"; and our worst troubles, which were menacing phantoms at bedtime, appear sometimes in the morning like the singing of birds. But the principal mercy of the arrangement is that it is a symbol. The Christian life is an awaking—a dressing; and each morning's waking and dressing may recall to us its nature.

Look at these verses carefully, and you will see the writer's meaning, though, with a true delicacy, he only hints at it.

When we rise from our beds we are dishevelled, unpresentable; we cannot get about the duties of the day until we have put off the dress of the night, until we have washed and combed ourselves, and put on a more suitable attire. Thus there is a surprising difference, in any nice and well-regulated person, between the night and the day appearance. The word "honestly" should rather be "decently," for it just expresses this difference.

The image is very homely, but it is saved from any touch of vulgarity by the noble idealism that pervades it:—" Let us cast off the works [not the mere dress] of darkness, and let us put on [not the mere clothes, but] the armour of light." Then it is suddenly raised to the highest level of allegorical dignity by the bold metaphor that Jesus Christ is Himself the garment which we are to put on.

I am thinking chiefly, just now, of the daily waking and dressing; but we must glance for a moment at the great fact of which this is the symbol, the reminder, the repetition.

Christ rose from the sleep of death, and in His resurrection body reassumed the glory that was His from the beginning. He rose, we are taught, "because our justification was accomplished." We believe in our justification, that we may rise with Him.

Are we risen with Him, or are we still in the drowsiness and the frowsiness of the night?

Here are certain specimen words which describe that nocturnal condition of the soul. The question hits us hard when we attempt to interpret them fairly.

First, REVELLINGS and DRUNKENNESS. This is not the boosing of the poor, who drink to forget their poverty and benumb their pain. It is the self-indulgence of the well-to-do. It includes the round of dinner-parties and dances, the repletion of good food, the hours spent over the pot or the decanter. It is the unhealthy occupation with these gaieties which makes them at last a craving, a necessity. A very large part of our English social life—parties which we affect to find " a bore," and yet are chagrined not to be invited to, all the hollow, insincere, trivial engagements which wither the life of the soul, and prevent us from putting on Christ Jesus—are included in this phrase, which we pharisaically confine to the intemperance of the poorer folk.

The CHAMBERINGS and WANTONNESS. These are the thoughts of our chambers, the wanton imagination on our beds, the loose fancies, the rein flung on the neck of passion. They are more important to mention than the overt acts of vice, for they are the letting-out of waters. Given these, the rest will follow—loose books, loose plays, loose company, the actual abominations of desolations; or, if the outward degradation does not get accomplished here, it is all one. The victims of chambering and wantonness are laying the foundations of lubricity and the unnameable in the world to come. These are "the provision of the flesh to fulfil the lusts thereof"; they are the steps down to the gates of death.

The last pair, STRIFE and
JEALOUSY, are as fatal to the reclothing in the Divine Garment,
Christ Jesus—as truly the unseemly dress of the night—as
those more scandalous faults which
are called vices. How poisonous
they are! A drunkard is more
tolerable than a quarreller. The
ruined victim of unclean indulgence is not more wretched than
one given to jealousy. These are
poisons at the springs of life.
They prohibit the indwelling of
the Spirit.

These three couplets of evil are
but specimen words—evil is manifold, protean, ubiquitous—but they
help us to answer the question,
Have we put off this "garment
spotted by the flesh"? Have we
taken up the "weapons of the
light," a sweet Abstinence, an inward Chastity, a Love before

which strife and jealousy melt away?

It was this searching passage that proved the turning-point in the life of Augustine. By the grace of God it may fetch any of us off our unhallowed couch and clothe us in the raiment of the day. It was at Milan, where the troubled spirit had come to seek help of the saintly Ambrose. He was with the brother Alypius in the garden. They had been reading the Epistles of Paul. Augustine rose in agitation and paced up and down, when he heard a clear child's voice singing from a house in the vicinity, "Take and read, take and read." As if commanded from heaven, he hastened back to the seat, and took up the book which they had been reading together. There was this verse staring him in the face. The Latin is "Not in feasts and tipplings, not in chambers and immodesties, not in contention and emulation; but put on the Lord Jesus Christ, and do not make provision for the flesh in concupiscence." The entrance of the word gave light. Presently, Alypius brought Augustine to Monica, to tell her that the mother's prayer was answered.

How many there are in England whose mother's prayers remain as yet unanswered; they lie abed; their religion is but "a dream within a dream"; it is of a piece with that experience, when, half awake, we dream that we have risen and washed and dressed; but, waking, we find that we have taken no step in that direction.

These words may be the *reveillé* to some slumbering soul.

But, assuming that we are in the great cardinal sense awakened and reclothed, still there remains the Daily Renewal of it, the parable of our diurnal round. We do not lie in bed unless we are ill. If we are spiritually well we truly arise every day. If we are bathed in the laver of regeneration, yet each day we need a washing of the hands and feet. Christ is a perfect garment, but it is necessary to put Him on afresh, readjust, and with loving care fit Him on, as the mornings come round.

But I can tell you better about this if I draw the portraits of two friends of mine. Their names are *Desidia* and *Alacritas*. The one dreams she is awake; the other is awake. You know them both, but it is odd how we often learn more from a portrait than from the original.

Desidia is not at all uncomely, but for a certain leaden and lethargic look in her eye and a drag in her gait. She begins the day with a very ample attention to her person. The time she spends on her hairdressing and her toilet would make three of her devotions, Sundays included. And her heart is in it, which I can hardly say about her devotions, notwithstanding her ivory-backed Prayer-book, which she carries very prettily to church as part of her elaborated costume. Her attachment to the Established Church is greatly cemented by this Prayer-book—"our beautiful liturgy," she calls it—and by the charming effect of a well-dressed congregation. If the ladies were not in the mode, and if the men were not in long frock coats with flowers at the button-hole, she could not worship. These are her "aids to devotion"; they are what Jeremy Taylor called

"The Golden Grove." I have said so much about her costume because she herself attaches so much importance to it. Yet I am not sure whether her dress is not out of fashion in Heaven these many years. Desidia has nothing particular to do, which is fortunate, for she never has time to do anything. I asked her once to undertake some work for her Saviour, which she refused so flatly that I ventured to inquire if He were her Saviour. It appeared that she was good enough to confess Him as her Saviour, and was quite undisturbed by a doubt whether He would at last confess her. It is a happy accident that the State of England has provided a Church to her liking, in which to be soothed by a good anthem and undisturbed by uncouth preaching is held to be a pretty preparation for Heaven.

But for this providence of the Church of England I have understood she would not be a Christian at all, and the world would go without the benefit of her religion. The only sad thing is that her state is exactly like that of the Five Foolish Virgins in the Parable.

Alacritas, on the other hand, always fills me with admiration; and I would gladly change my sex to be like her. She is never in a hurry, and yet is always moving. She has so much merriment and gaiety of heart that grave, religious folk at first take exception to her, and question whether a true Christian could ever have so exchanged the spirit of heaviness for the garment of praise. But I chance to know that this sunshine comes from prayer, and it is like a good medicine in the house; for, as the wise man says, "A merry heart causeth good healing." I never can make out how she gets so much time. The day for her appears to be stretched. Her sun does not go down; the moon for her stands still in the valley of Ajalon. It may be my bad taste, but I am mightily taken with her dress. I should have thought it would take twice as long to get oneself up so charmingly as Alacritas does—I mean as compared with the artificial fripperies of Desidia. Yet Alacritas gets a good hour for prayer before breakfast; she does a great deal of household work, she visits the poor, and her needle is busy for them; she never seems to miss a service at the church. And yet she reads more good literature in a month than Desidia does in a year.

Desidia and others of her family

pity Alacritas because she has little or nothing to do with Plays and Dances. How dull it must be for her, they say. I fairly laughed the last time Desidia bestirred herself from her habitual *ennui* and boredom to make this remark to me.

The truth is, Alacritas belongs to those spoken of by the prophet:

Out of them shall proceed thanksgiving and the voice of them that make merry.

And the same prophet has spoken more particularly about *her*:

Thou shalt be built, O Virgin of Israel; thou shalt be adorned with thy tabrets, and shalt go forth in the dances of them that make merry.

And yet once more, through the same prophet, her Lord has said of her:

Yea, I have loved thee with an everlasting love, therefore with loving-kindness have I drawn thee.—(JER. xxx. 19; xxxi. 4, 3.)

The Garden of Lilies.

> My beloved is gone to his garden.
> He feedeth his flock among the lilies.
> —CANTICLES VI. 2, 3.

MANY things have been said in praise of gardens, especially in the older days when land was plentiful, and the houses, even of cities, were not so impertinently crowded together as they are to-day. It is the first and most obvious joy of living in the country that, even with small means, you may have your own garden. It is one of the most irremediable deprivations of the town that, even with considerable means, you cannot get that simple luxury. What is the use of large rooms and well furnished, when you have not a garden?

Now, the special delight of a garden is twofold; first, you have there a piece of Nature brought home to your heart; second, you can have a hand in her operations, and therefore feel more intimately their wonder and loveliness.

You have a piece of Nature brought home to your heart. For Nature is vast and varied, too inapprehensible for minds which cannot be given wholly to her, exigent rather than restful in her illimitable range. But in your garden she steals to your feet, to be touched and loved and understood. You can sit at leisure with her and put your hand in hers. She turns to you her homely side. Her mountain heights, her roaring cataracts, her tremendous seas, her wild profusion of fauna and flora, are hushed and tempered in the gentle slope of the lawn, the quiet patter of the rain, the drenching dews of cloudy nights, the thrushes making their morning meal, the flowering plants which you have planted yourself. For this is your second delight, that you have a hand in her operations. You can smell the quickening scent of fresh-turned soil; you can watch the seedlings peering above the ground; you can decorate your rooms with flowers of your own growing; you can, like primitive man, furnish your table with fruits and vegetables which have ripened under your own watchful eyes.

Now a Christian church is not inaptly compared to a garden; a church, I mean, such as we Congregationalists understand it. *The* Church, that vast invisible and visible Society which is spoken of in the *Ephesians*, is too vast and varied for practical realisation. It is an inspiring and invigorating idea, and to lose sight of its catholicity is a loss very similar to that of being for ever shut out from Nature's largest and most magnificent doings. The Brotherhood of Man is the noblest of thoughts, but it must be interpreted by actual brotherhood with *men*. The music of the Spheres may be the secret of all music, but we want sounds which we can hear as well. We may worship with invisible choirs; but not so well as if we have some visible choir in which we tune our preludes. Now the individual church which we enter as members is a piece of The Church brought home to our heart. Here the mighty worship of the invisible choirs is rendered audible for us and by us. Here the vast Christian ideas, the brotherhood, the mutual service, the united effort for the Kingdom of God, are translated into practical realities. Here we arrest the vague assertion, "I believe in the communion of saints," which is apt to become mere sentiment, with the importunate demand to practise that communion with these saints who are at your side, at your heart.

Here, too, you get your hand into the great operations of the Church. Here you sow your seeds, bed out your plants, watch them, water them, cherish them. Here you get your little harvests, which are foretastes of the great harvest, in the souls redeemed and trained and purified. Here you find your rest and your refreshment, your springtime and your harvest. Melodious sounds wake the morning and usher in the evening. And the sense of ingathering comforts the heart wearied with the world.

O sound to rout the brood of cares,
    The sweep of scythe in morning dew,
    The gust which round the garden blew,
And tumbled half the mellowing pears.

But this is called a garden of lilies. I shall entertain you with no botanical discussion about the species of this plant. More to my point is a suggestion from this description given by Mme. Darmesteter of hunting stags in the woods of Valois:

Every May a beautiful fault frustrates this skilful venery; for thick as grass, thick and sweet, the lily of the valley springs in all the brakes and shady places. The scent of the game will not lie across these miles of blossom. The hunters are in despair, and the deer, who sets his back against the sturdiest oak and butts at the pack with his antlers, who swims the lake, and from his island refuge sells his life as hard as he can— the deer, accustomed to be always vanquished, beholds himself at last befriended by an ally more invincible than water or forest oak, by the sweet innumerable white lily, innocent as himself, that every Maytime sends the huntsman home.

Now, when I speak of the church, the Congregational church-community, as a garden of lilies, I am thinking not only of delight, but of protection, not only of sweetness, but of safety. I am aware that many men, most men, are like hunted deer, who need a refuge. Brave stands they make against the hounds of care, and the cruel huntsmen of the tempter; they sell their lives dearly, but ultimately they succumb. That is no real church to them that does not afford a place of escape, where the sweet odours of love and trust and comprehension baffle the pursuer. I do not know what has come over some of the churches, or what they suppose they exist for. The lilies are all dead, and if a harassed man takes refuge in their borders, he will fall an immediate prey to the dogs and the tempter, who hunts nowhere else with more security or certainty of success than within their borders.

It would seem, therefore, to be the first question to put concerning any church, Do the lilies of love blossom there, and is their odour wafted abroad on every breeze that blows?

But I am impatient to speak to you about "our Beloved, who has gone down into His garden to the beds of spices, and feedeth His flock among the lilies."

It is the presence of Christ in a church which alone makes it capable of fulfilling its functions. Has He or has He not gone down into this garden of His? The answer will be furnished by a crowd of most palpable facts. It is said of the neo-Catholic writers, such as Newman and Ward, that "they have marvellously little to say about Christ. It is the Church, the Church, the Church. No doubt they would say that, in speaking of the Church, they implied Christ's presence. But such a matter ought not to be left to implication." Talk about Christ and His personal presence, and the Church will follow naturally, so as to make it clear that without Him there will be no Church. But talk about the Church always, and while you are talking you will find that He has slipped out at the postern-gate. I recollect a well-to-do Congregationalist complaining to me that at his chapel it was all Christ, Christ, Christ, until he was tired of it. I was informed a short time after that he had entered the Established Church. Curious, that we do not notice how often men flee into " the Church " to escape from Christ. There are churches impenetrably barred against Him; you are more likely to meet Him in a large warehouse, on 'Change, in the House of Commons, than in them. Such churches will be popular with Dives, but useless to Lazarus. The tempted, the tried, the troubled, precisely those in whom Christ has the deepest interet, will never enter their gates, or entering, will flee, as from the mockery of a refuge.

Now let us lay down some very plain and obvious principles—(1)

about the effects of His presence in a church; (2) about the means of securing His presence. Or, in other words, let me first praise the spiritual garden, then notice how it may be filled with lilies.

I. Christ's presence in a church implies:

(1) *Expansion*. There must be added to it continually such as are being saved. When He is lifted up He draws men to Him. The neighbourhood is decaying, we say. Does that mean it is becoming depopulated, or that all the people are Christians? Usually, it means the reverse. Christ's presence in the midst of a decaying neighbourhood means a garden of Eden in the midst of the desolation; and the precious aroma and gleam of the garden will be as attractive to the poor decaying souls as a garden of the Hesperides

would be to the city urchins who press their cheeks against its iron bars and seek to climb its walls. Or the neighbourhood is over-churched, and there are not people to be drawn in. No, but Christ's presence will mean that the children of the families are being drawn to Him. Crowds are nothing. Little children and stragglers by ones and twos come to Him in the early morning or in the dark evening of life. And a church which is hampered and cramped by its immediate surroundings will be specially concerned with the regions beyond, the vast stretches of heathendom demanding workers and consecrated lives. I notice that missionaries are, like Livingstone, very generally called from these small and apparently hindbound churches. Christ's presence sends the members far off among the heathen.

(2) *Prayer.* The Son of Man was the most prayerful among the sons of men. And His presence is always gathering the two or three together to realise it. Some seem to think that you must pray to get Him; but, that when He is got, the prayer-meeting may be given up, and the members may stay away. Others know better, for they accept and realise His presence by prayer, and to cease praying because He has come would be like hiding the flowers under the soil because they have reared their heads above it, or wooing the songbirds into the boughs in order to snare and to silence them.

Christ's presence gives the power of that continuous and importunate prayer which Christ's lips taught us is the condition of all real blessing. When you observe that there is no interest in prayer, no wish to assemble for the purpose, no quickness in opening the lips, no unction in petition, no soaring faith in the requests and the aspirations, you may be sure that a keen eye would see the skirt of the robe of Christ just quitting the unhallowed gates. You know where Christ has been by these flowers of prayer that spring up everywhere at His feet.

(3) *Love.* Now, love is in most of us like a sealed spring. It would flow well enough if the stone at the mouth were removed. It would not do to conclude, when you see a church of stiff, self-centred people, who never go out to one another, never concern themselves with the sorrows or joys of their neighbours, never sacrifice themselves for anything

except their own unpleasurable pleasures, that these are sinners beyond all that dwell in Zion, or are made of a different clay from the rest of mankind. You can only conclude that the seal has never yet been taken off the fountain — it remains unbroken. They have come into no personal contact with the crucified Christ— never, except in hymns and idle emotion, did they see from His hands, His face,

   Sorrow and love flow mingled down.

I fear sometimes the delicate veils of our sermons hide Christ from the church. Something, at any rate, hides Him. These dear souls never saw Him. But supposing He is really manifested in the church, not now and then, but habitually, the seal breaks. They feel the fountain rising within them, flowing out towards Him, a strong devotion, the impulse of sacrifice. And from the opened fountain the crystal tide flows around. When you have looked on Christ with love, you look on His brethren with love. It is impossible to be indifferent to those who are called by His name. They may not be naturally attractive, but they attract far more than natural attractions do. The magic of His presence has passed into them. It is easy to be patient, considerate, serviceable to people in whom you never know but that you may be touching Christ; just as the gold miner will handle the rough quartz with the keenest interest, and take any pains to get at its centre, believing that gold is there.

And love set flowing in a church never stops with the church, but is like the stream which issued from the Temple and flowed towards the sunrise in Ezekiel's vision.

But we must turn now from that happy and endless enumeration of the results which follow from the presence of Christ in His garden, to consider how we can make our garden a garden of lilies by securing His continual presence.

II. *How can we keep Christ in His Church?* Now, I am not of those who underrate the mystical elements in our religion, nor am I tempted to depreciate the emotional experiences which accompany a true and active faith. But the conviction grows on me that the mystical and the emotional do not come first. To reach the point of a mystical intercourse with God there is for us, as for Moses and Elijah, a barren desert to be patiently crossed, a rugged mountain to be laboriously climbed.

To enter into the ecstasy of Christian joy—which is to be found on the upper platform of the Temple—there are degrees or steps which have to be mounted. There is no real entrance but by the staircase and the door; as you may often see on a Sunday morning when a congregation listlessly assembles and flings itself idly into singing and praying and listening without an effort to really enter into the courts of the Lord, or to ascend the golden ladder which connects earth and heaven.

Before mysticism comes action, before emotion duty. And to this point we cannot too solemnly recall the wandering attention of the Church.

I am tired of hearing the Christian law treated as if it dealt only with negatives and prohibitions. That was the Judaism which Christ superseded. "Thou shalt not," leaves always the true second table of the law untouched. That second table runs throughout "Thou shalt." And principally and summarily it is, Thou shalt love the Lord thy God with all thy heart and mind, and thou shalt love thy neighbour as thyself.

If a church is bent on securing the constant presence of Christ it must proceed in the most business-like way to carry out His commandments. Here, at any rate, there are no rights without duties. The attempt to claim the privileges without discharging the tasks of the Church is the source of all confusion, and the certain way to drive Christ forth of His own doors.

Shall we briefly state the positive commands—the true Decalogue of the Christian Church, the observance of which retains our Lord in the midst approving and blessing, the breach of which renders His presence, if He is there at all, merely a condemnation and a torture?

First: Thou shalt believe in the Lord Jesus Christ, trust Him, be assured in Him.

Second: Thou shalt confess Him before men, and leave no one in doubt where thou standest.

Third: Thou shalt receive the Holy Ghost, and proceed to live, not in the flesh, but in the Spirit.

Fourth: Thou shalt seek first the Kingdom of God by thyself obeying and by bringing others to obedience.

Fifth: Thou shalt lovingly minister to every suffering fellow-creature whom thou canst reach, believing that whatsoever thou doest to these thou doest to Christ.

Sixth: You shall assemble together, remembering that you are a body of Christ.

Seventh: Walking in the light you shall have fellowship with one another.

Eighth: You shall bear one another's burdens instead of your own.

Ninth: You shall exercise for one another's benefit the gifts of the Spirit entrusted to you.

Tenth: You shall go into the whole world and preach the Gospel to every creature.

Now, no one questions that a garden uncultivated is no garden at all. I would rather have the wild moorland and the lovely desolation of the elements than a garden with the hedges trodden down, the pathways grown over with grass and the beds unclean with weeds. And this is the secret of the world's scorn directed against the churches. The neglected garden is a reproach and an eyesore.

The members of a church have therefore a great co-operative task to cultivate their garden, and they must pass from the Decalogue of the Old Testament to the Decalogue of the New. By the punctual observance of these commandments which our Beloved has given to us, we shall win His presence, and where He comes the sweet lilies blow; and as if He were Himself the Vine, the branches bear abundant fruit.

A Call to Work.

Acts xxvi.

This chapter teems with instruction for Christian men and women directly they will recognise that St. Paul is not presented to us as an exception, but as an example of what every Christ-filled man should be. We are apt to look at the apostles too much in the halo and the nimbus which the Art and the reverence of ages have thrown around them, and to forget that they are men of like passions with ourselves.

Here are (1) The commission of a Christian; (2) An instance of its fulfilment.

(1) This man relates before

Festus, the Roman Governor, and Herod Agrippa, the King, how he came into contact with the Risen Christ, and was called by Him to the work of his life. Christ says to Paul, "I send thee" (v. 18). Beyond all question the secret of Christian service is a fact of this kind at the root of the Christian life; and the absence of this fact is the explanation of the failure which marks so much professional religious work. We can do little or nothing while we are apologising for Christ, and trying to persuade ourselves, by persuading others, that there is a Christ at all. Nay, we cannot do much even when our conviction of His existence, His beauty, His power, His love, has become quite genuine and forcible. All our work halts until He has given His commission to us, and we appear simply as His ambassadors, with our letters royal signed and sealed in our own experience, the *I send thee* of our appointment. It is very pathetic to see well-meaning men moiling and toiling for the advancement of the Kingdom, and yet to hear the distinct voice of Jesus, "I did not send them; they speak in their own name, and not in Mine."

Paul was certainly a forceful character. His admirable energy in exterminating the Christians while he thought them wrong throws a flood of light on his natural resolution and pertinacity. Without any false modesty, we may protest that we are by no means the equals of this active and fiery spirit. But the only reason why we are speaking of Paul to-day, the only explanation of the wide influence which he seems to be still exerting in the world, lies in this phrase, *I send thee.* It is the Christ behind Paul that makes him significant. And we who are by nature less gifted, less remarkable, may still more expect to find our sole power, our sole significance, our sole helpfulness for the world in that condition. Has Christ appeared to us by the way and said, "I send you"?

The commission grows out of the experience. The man's eyes were opened there on the road to Damascus, and accordingly he is sent to open men's eyes. If he had not seen Jesus, he would have been a poor operator for showing Jesus to others. It is the world's great sorrow at present that for one reason or another the eyes of so many are held that they cannot see HIM. Men are sorely needed who have seen Him. Holman Hunt saw Him, and painted that wonderful picture "The Light of the World," and he says, in speaking of that ravishing vision, "Renan's works I have read exhaustively; they are, spite of the scholarship which makes them worth reading, simply puerile nonsense, with about as much knowledge of his subject as Payne Knight had of the Elgin marbles." That sounds strong, but what can we say? Fancy an artist trying to paint a portrait without seeing his subject—nay, fancy a judge passing sentence even on a criminal without having him before the bar. And in much of the present talk about Jesus, in the writings of some very able men, in the teaching even of some professedly Christian ministers, one is constrained to cry out, "Why they are depicting One whom they have never seen. They are trying to open men's eyes, and their own are closed."

He sends us—this radiant, risen Lord—sends us to open men's eyes to see Him. And by what methods does He expect it to be done? I believe the chief method is *prayer*. Ananias was evidently in prayer when he was sent to open the eyes of Paul himself. And Paul, in his turn, says that in prayer he sought for his friends that the God of our Lord Jesus Christ would give them a spirit of wisdom and revelation in the knowledge of Him, having the eyes of their heart enlightened (Eph. i. 17, 18). Another method is *preaching;* before the eyes of the Galatians Paul openly set forth Jesus Christ crucified (Gal. iii. 1), and a faithful, earnest presentation of Jesus from week to week has a remarkable effect in opening men's eyes, gradually or suddenly; and when we get tired of setting forth Christ, their eyes close again. But another excellent method of opening the eyes is to *live* Christ. A man came from Ningpo to a missionary to be baptized, and was asked where he had heard the Gospel. "Oh," he said, "I have never heard the Gospel, but I have *seen* it; there was an opium smoker in Ningpo with a bad temper, who learned about the Christian religion, and his whole life became changed." Perhaps nothing opens eyes more than this.

And when men's eyes are open to see Jesus, they see at a glance God and themselves; they see their own position, and they see God's relation to them. And what is the result? They turn from darkness to light, from the power of Satan unto God; they receive remission of sins, and an inheritance among those who are sanctified by faith in Jesus. We need not think of men as wilfully bad—they are, as a rule, only blind, deluded, in the dark. When all these Agnostics say that they see no evidence of God, of Christ, of salvation, I believe them; I am sure they do not see, or they would turn. When these poor creatures hand themselves over to vice, to covetousness, to selfishness, one knows at once it must be blindness. Who would walk into the Gate of Hell with his eyes open, or embrace Satan, knowing it to be Satan? And when the multitude of the indifferent live without God and without hope in the world, who can question that it is because their eyes are closed? If the unfortunates were not blind they would never choose the dark and darkening lot which is theirs instead of the inheritance among the saints in light, the sanctification which is through faith in Christ.

(2) *An instance of fulfilling the commission.* With this commission to open men's eyes in our hands common compassion impels us to miss voluntarily no opportunity. Paul was not in the habit of waiting for a pulpit or a set meeting. Where he found blind eyes he tried at once to open them. Agrippa did not seem a likely subject—the petty tetrarch to whom Claudius had granted the title of king, the representative of the perverse Herods, weak and worldly, combining the faults of Jew and Gentile, of Greek and Roman. And by his side was his sister, Bernice, who had been the wife of her uncle, was now the wife of her brother, and afterwards be-

came the mistress of Vespasian. Besides, Paul was before him as a prisoner before a judge, not as a preacher before a congregation. There is no better instance of being active and aggressive in season and out of season. Paul proceeds, in his eager, vehement way, to grapple with the king, to appeal to him as a Jew. He will start from the prophets. If he can get Agrippa's confession of faith in them, he will quickly land him at the Cross and the Risen Christ, as the discourses in this book show again and again. Agrippa seems to see what will happen, and with a rebuke, half-scornful, but perhaps half-regretful, he says: "This is persuasion by short-cuts to make me a Christian." What an outburst of passionate longing the remark evoked from this shackled prisoner. "I would pray to God that by short cut or long you and all these might be as I am, but for these fetters!" There is the secret of the Christian heart. Such is the experience of Christ that, notwithstanding all sufferings and drawbacks, it would have all the world like itself. As Christ enters and possesses a human soul, it becomes a burning centre of desire and effort to bring every one else to Him.

We are told that the present Empress of China summoned a tailor in Pekin to make her a wedding-dress; and the man was a Christian, who seized the opportunity to present Christ to her, and asked her to accept a New Testament. He was but a poor exponent of the faith, but he persuaded her to hear a young Chinese gentleman who was studying at the Mission College. The effort was not apparently more successful than this appeal of Paul's to Agrippa. But we have nothing to do with success. Our Lord sends us as witnesses in season and out of season. It behoves us to be about His business, to joyfully deliver His testimony and leave the issue with Him.

There appeared in the papers, the other day, an account of a monk who, finding the hollowness of the Monastic method of salvation, sought the help of some ritualist priest, who urged him to submit to his Church. Led by a strange accident, he then came to the house of a Presbyterian minister, who was out at the time. But the minister's wife saw the perplexed inquirer, and seized the opportunity to present Christ as the perfect and present Saviour to him. He saw, and believed. We need all to be similarly alert. We leave too much to the minister. It is not his business any more than yours to open men's eyes to Jesus; every one who has seen the Lord is sent to show Him to others.

Indeed, one of the chief duties of the minister is to keep ever before his people the reality of their own commission, and to urge and counsel them with all affectionate suggestion and shining example, to move everywhere in life as the Sent of Jesus, persuading men with all summariness to become Christians, turning them from darkness to light, leading them to forgiveness, and securing for them an inheritance among the sanctified.

The Meaning of Spring.

I ALWAYS feel aggrieved, though doubtless I, and I alone, am to blame, that, seeing each man can have only seventy Springs or so in his life, I was allowed to pass more than half of my allotted number, and no man pointed out to me the meaning of the Spring. Doubtless it was my own fault. Poets and preachers were telling me all the time, but I was too dull to understand. I found out the glory of an English Spring—as one finds out so much of the glory in the universe—by having to forego it for once. It was in 1893 that I was obliged to leave an English Spring, to cross the Atlantic to a Springless land.

Daily the vain cry was in my heart:

Oh, to be in England
Now that April's there.
And whoever wakes in England
Sees, some morning, unaware,
That the lowest boughs and the brush-
  wood sheaf
Round the elm-tree bole are in tiny leaf,
While the chaffinch sings on the orchard
  bough
In England, now!

Yes; I found in 1893 the glory of the English Spring, by leaving it. But the meaning of the Spring I did not find even then.

Of course, I am not speaking of the beauty. The beauty of the Spring we have all felt since childhood—the affluence of flowers, the snow-fall of the fruit blossoms in the orchard, the curious sense of response in Nature to what is passing within. Yes; in our life's time of Spring, Spring spoke to us as it cannot now. We fell into a harmony with it. It was the one season in the year when the courses of our blood and the courses of nature chimed. And in each succeeding stage of life we have not failed of the beauty of the Spring; its tenderness appealed to our youth, its promise to our manhood, its pensive transitiveness to our maturity, its breath of resurrection to our decay. None of us can charge himself with being insensible to a beauty which masters the world.

But what I missed until lately was the *meaning* of Spring, its sacramental meaning — the sense in which, *ex opere operato*, it confers grace on the soul, takes the believing heart by storm, and carries inward the ineffable realities, the nutriment of God.

I suspect we miss this truth because we are too eager to treat the season as a Parable, to point a moral, to illustrate a spiritual doctrine. Parable it is, no doubt. Our Lord used it as a parable, as He watched the Sower on the hillside, and when, while it wanted three months to harvest, He saw the world awaiting for His Spring-messengers with their scattered grain. But while we are eager to use the matter allegorically, and to find a lesson of analogy which may lie behind, we are likely enough to miss the matter, and, while anxious to impart through an illustration a spiritual and moral truth, to overlook the religious directness of the illustration itself.

It seemed easier for our pre-Christian fathers than for us to let the world speak its own language to them. The Spring among the Greeks gave a religious message, because no one wished to use it for secondary purposes. Persephone plucked the flowers on the pleasant lea of Sicily, and Dis, the god of the under-world, was smitten with her beauty. He rapt her, flowers and all, into his gloomy regions. And Demeter, her mother, passed sorrowfully over the tilths, into the farm-houses and the hamlets, always mourning the loss of her daughter until she should for the brief Spring months be restored. Thus, the Greek read out of the Spring, so loved, so early lost, so passionately desired, the pathos of human life, the longing of the bereaved, the recovery of the departed.

But until Wordsworth came no Christian seemed able to reclaim all the simplicity and directness, all the Divine significance of

The Pagan creed outworn.

Many drew lessons from the Spring, but no one encouraged us in the frank Hellenic way to hear the Spring's own lesson, to let *it* speak to us.

Now, here is the Sacramental meaning of the Spring, not remote or difficult, but close at hand and plain. The Spring, as we have it here in England, is, in the simplest possible way, God manifesting Himself immediately to every one who has an eye and a heart and a susceptibility for the Divine, manifesting Himself, not as in Scripture, for didactic purposes, not to convey an ethical monition, or an ulterior spiritual truth, but showing Himself in the exuberance of His own rich and exhaustless being, so that if one is envious to know what God in His nature is, what passes through His mind, what kind of joy nestles at His heart, what raptures thrill Him, what curious purposes shape themselves and push to their goal, it is possible to see, all very plainly revealed.

And consider, if He wishes to explain to a trained sensibility what He is like; if He would permit an eye to observe or a hand to touch; if He would encourage a mind to estimate the processes of His being,—how should He better show the shy secret, suggest the unutterable truth, than by this kind of restrained and delicate prodigality? It is all exhaustless, infinitely varied, but yet how fine, how tempered, like the most spiritual touch of the brush with the shadowy suggestions of the mysteries of the palette! That faint film of green flung like a gauze veil over the palpitating breasts of the trees; that rapturous freshness of the young vegetation underfoot; that wild profusion of flowers, and the colours of them, the frail white and veined pink of anemones and wood sorrel, the pale yellow, as of sunrise skies, the joyous orange belts of primrose and cowslip, the first music of bluebells, the white of the fruit blossoms. There is nothing red as yet, nothing loud, demonstrative, open-bosomed. It is all thrilling with tender hope, the sweet shades that rest and rejoice, but never satiate or pall. Then, that clarity of the light, the twinkle of unoppressive sunshine, and if you can be near them, the wreathed morning mists on the mountains and the blue shimmer of the early sea. And for crown of joy and chorus of blessing these doings of the birds. The lark is up taking his messages to God and fetching them back. The blackbird drops his deliberate staves of liquid music from the top bough of the opening lilac. The cheerful bar of the tits awakes the morn, and the long rapture of the nightingale maintains that to His sleeping world God is still speaking, singing songs in the night while they sleep.

But there is a whole which is more than the analysed parts. In the whole He lays a Divine hand on us, and says, gently and musically, It is I.

* * * * *

The hand is quickly withdrawn. Alas! the brevity exhausts us with desire. How can we drink it all in, or enjoy it before it is gone? But the quick withdrawal is a large part of the meaning. The hand withdrawn becomes one which beckons. It beckons to a land, a world which you will never believe in if you do not believe in Spring, and which God cannot tell you of if this will not convince you—

There everlasting Spring abides, and
    never withering flowers,
Sweet fields beyond the swelling floods
    stand dressed in living green.

That is Watts at his best. It is religion at its best. It takes the best of life, of the world, eternises it, flings it into the invisible, and calls it heaven. Surely it is a true method. In all this loveliness and joy is sheathed a promise. The fleeting ecstacy of Spring speaks better things than the permanent joys of the world. It promises that we

    Shall recapture
This first fine careless rapture.

Nor is it mere feeling. There is a valid argument in it; for if

> Nature never did betray the heart that loved her,

certainly God will not betray the heart that loves Him. But Nature would betray our hearts if Spring did not speak of "everlasting Spring and never withering flowers." She would have mocked us in our tenderest mood, which was her own creation. And if all this pageant of the Spring is simply God manifesting Himself, still more sure is the word of prophecy. Holy men of old spake as they were moved by the Spirit; so Spring speaks, and she speaks only of love, of resurrection, and of a heart which even she does not fully express.

On Getting Out of Ruts.

THERE is in Deut. iv. 25 one of those Hebrew words which defy translation into English, for the English rendering, "have been long in the land," is so tame and placid that it cannot claim to represent the original at all. It is an idiomatic peculiarity in Hebrew to employ a verb when we should express the thought by an adjective and the copula; that is to say, there will be a verb to express the idea "I am old," or "I have become old." In the present instance we have a root which signifies "languor," and out of it is coined a verb which means "to be languid," or in another mood, to have become languid. This verb in the participle occurs, for instance, in Levit. xxvi. 10, where it is rendered by "old store long kept." One might say "exhausted" food, food which has lost its vital element, and is insipid and shrivelled. Not inappropriately the word is used of a leprosy, in Levit. xiii. 2. The blighting, withering, corroding disease has settled down in the flesh. It masters the body with the *vis inertiæ* of death. This same word occurs in Deut. iv. 25, with people as the subject. To render the idea of this single Hebrew word, a long paraphrase is needed. Let us try to supply it. "When thou shalt beget children, and children's children, and ye shall have settled in the land until the torpor of custom has crept over you, and the gangrene of inveterate stagnation has made you like a disease in the land, when the vital elements in you have gone to sleep, and you have become like the body of this death, and shall corrupt yourselves, &c." It is from such a condition in life, or death in life, that idolatry springs. Men in this state make idols like unto themselves. Just as living men worship the living God, so men who have become stocks and stones worship stocks and stones. As we assimilate ourselves with the old *débris*, the scrofulous scurf, the ancient gangrene of the earth, we lose touch with God. We are transformed into the likeness of the inanimate and unmoving things. We are surprised, like the people of Greek mythology, in the act of passing into shrubs or statues of stone. Daphne is changed into the laurel; they who see the Gorgon's head turn into stone. In this unhappy degeneracy we observe the blood depart from our lips, as the pallor of marble creeps over them, and find our supple and sentient limbs stiffening into the fibrous branches of trees.

And this disastrous change is due simply to what for want of a better word we must call *inveteracy*. You shall go on doing the same things, not bad things in themselves, over and over again; getting up in the morning, uttering your formal prayers, shuffling through the accustomed duties of the day, undressing, praying, and falling asleep at night; once a week you shall go to the house of worship, with the same deadening sensations, sit in the same pew, drowse through the same service, duck your head in the same attitude of prayer; you shall go through the same routine of religious duties, visiting, attending committees, teaching; you shall read the same newspapers and books, and repeat the same ideas to the people at the table with you or in the street or warehouse; until by a process which might be that of witchcraft, you find that the savour, the vital juice, the animation, has gone out of everything. Surely you are bewitched!

There in the old cromlech, opened unexpectedly to the light, lie the records and relics of men long passed away. Observe that ancient sword which lies by what was once the skeleton of a man, the skeleton itself long since resolved into dust. Handle, hilt and blade, it is all there, red and eaten with rust, the point and edge still discernible, a sword surely, though no longer an efficient sword. But grasp the handle, it comes away; touch the edge, it crumbles. The implement lies only in the semblance of a sword. It cannot bear the contact of a human hand, fallen to pieces, settled in inveterate decay and corruption by the lapse of centuries.

> His strong blade, Toledo trusty,
> For lack of using had grown rusty.

It is that kind of fate which befalls the soul and the church and all things human. Things retain their appearance *in situ*. Move them, and they fall into dust. The vital fluid has withdrawn. The particles of matter have lost their cohesion, they are only in the ghostly form of things, and await the disturbing hand of time which will dissipate even the ghosts. We may easily become "inveterate" in the land, like a crumbled castle that stands in the memory of sieges and the reputation of impregnability, until the first shot from a gun or the shock of an explosion reveals that it is but a shadow of strength.

Shelley has a weird sonnet on Ozymandias, which tells of a traveller's report from the desert. "Two vast and trunkless legs of stone" stood there, and by their side the shattered visage still retained the cold, scornful features of the great king; and on the pedestal these words:

My name is Ozymandias, King of Kings.
Look on my works, ye mighty, and despair!

And the poem ends:

Nothing beside remains. Round the decay

Of that colossal wreck, boundless and bare,
The lone and level sands stretch far away.

That is the inveteracy of what has been in the land, the hollow and meaningless echo of a life that was, the vaunt become too ludicrous yet too pathetic for laughter or for tears. The main purpose of holidays should be not so much to recruit our physical powers as to raise our souls from the ruts, and save them from the impending peril of inveteracy. Our churches, like ourselves, have a natural and steady tendency towards the idolatry of habit. Reformations and cataclysms are often necessary to save them from their fate. Your Romanism becomes in the course of ages the insensible absorption of every element of Paganism. Your Pope is the Pontifex Maximus of the heathen religion. Your Peter whose toe you kiss is the statue of Jupiter Capitolinus. Your vestments and rites steal back into Christianity from the gay and godless religion which it dispossessed. Your gods and goddesses return as saints and virgins. The old shrines serve, the old festivals are kept, the old names are easily altered. And presently your Christianity promising fair to effect the regeneration of the world, is simply the old world-religion mastering and nullifying the great new Evangel. Your Independency is not exempt from the same inherent tendencies. Your minister sinks into the familiar priest of the high places and the shrines. Your extemporary prayers become liturgies without the majesty or the grace. Your popular government drifts into a bureaucracy; your

ON GETTING OUT OF RUTS. 93

sacred church meeting becomes not very different from a vestry meeting. Your church, almost insensibly, has become an edifice of conventions, into which the world as we know it, the live, striving, actual world will not enter. Your tone has become professional. Your services are customs.

Cataclysms and revolutions may be necessary for salvation.

The old order changeth, yielding place
   to new,
And God fulfils Himself in many ways,
Lest one good custom should corrupt the
   world.

But holidays rightly used might spare us revolutions. From year to year we might become fresh and strong. Each summer we might acquire the old, childlike look at things. Out of the ruts we might learn to move, to see and feel as we did in the dewy dawn of life. How to use our holidays for such a purpose is a question of great pith and moment. And certainly God has prepared an earth and settled the ordinances of heaven, in a way adapted to effect this result. Leave the mere city and its civilities behind; hush the long drawl and the weary cant of common life; come away where there is no builder but God, where the heavens can settle on your spirit, where the eternal evolution breaks and forgets all transient and transitional forms.

It is surely a species of mania which drives the unhappy English to mean by a holiday the exact transference of all their daily habits and prejudices into another country for a few weeks in the summer. Instead of escaping from their cage for a flight over summer seas they take their cage with them, and get as tightly shut into it as the obliging foreigner will allow. I could laugh and weep, too, when I see these dreary souls away from home. They had a tennis-court at home; therefore they must have it abroad, though it be on a mountain side, or on the dunes of the sea. They spend their days at home in idle social functions; therefore they can make nothing of a holiday which does not give them repeated changes of dress, gossip, and the adored formalities. Their only idea of worship is hearing the English Prayer-book intoned, and seeing a priest in certain vestments wag his pow in the pulpit. Good heavens! they might in their holidays get a notion of that grand truth that Christianity is not confined to the Church of England,

and God can be approached without the offices of a curate. But no; whether in a lonely hotel on a Swiss mountain, or in the religious heart of Norway, they must have their church, their Prayer-book, their chaplain. Their Church is the Church of England, their God is the God of England; outside of England He cannot be found unless one can make believe with Prayer-book, chaplain and vestments, that a load of the sacred soil has been carried out into the godless lands.

Surely it is a very Midsummer madness. It is this which corrupts our people and leads them insensibly into making a graven image. Instead of seeking to escape from the inveteracy, they are particular to carry it from their ordinary life through their holidays with the same unyielding

ON GETTING OUT OF RUTS.

pertinacity. Unhappy English! Supposing Heaven should be a land unlike English Society, where English customs and liturgies and other insularities are intrinsically impossible? Surely it would be well to take into account that, if not made fit for heaven, we at least need to be loosened from earth to make any joyful entrance there. Now, if the holidays are to serve in any degree to lift us out of the ruts, and to set us in a free and flexible way to approach God and carry out His will, we should certainly use them for those purposes which are baulked by the ordinary habits of our life. That is to say, we should try to realise other kinds of men and other ways of living, other interpretations of religion, and other methods of Christian practice. Instead of carrying our chaplain and his carpet-bag of vestments with us, we should worship with the people among whom we are sojourning. Most countries we journey in are Christian countries; and most heathen countries offer a better worship than I have frequently found at Continental Chaplaincies. Some of our people might effectually break the routine of their lives in their holidays by going to church anywhere; it would be the greatest change, the most remarkable refreshment to go to service twice a Sunday for three weeks running.

But then, again, what most of us miss in our city life is the unreserved contact with nature. How large secrets she would readily communicate to all, but she is not able to do it to people who make a rush for the train in the morning, plunge into the newspaper, drag through feverish hours of business, and return exhausted and choked to a sleepy evening. The holidays are Nature's chance with certain hearts that love her. That is one great reason for going to the sea. Man has well-nigh driven nature off the land with a pitchfork, and has thrust his deforming trivialities right down to the shore and out to the pierheads; but there his power ceases. You may fix your eyes on the sea and become absorbed in primal, unspoiled Nature. The thrill of her vastness and strength will pass through you. The excitements and sick hurries of life will immediately be forgotten. In the lapping of those brooding waves, or in their long-drawn thunder, in the far distances and the shifting hues, traversed by solitary sunlit sails, you will be assimilated with—

> The Mighty Being, which doth make
> A noise like thunder everlastingly!

After some intercourse with the sea, gazing on it, listening to it, plunging into it, one may return a new creature for new enterprises.

But every wise man knows that the first need of life is some draught at the perennial springs of God. The trite ways of life, the lulling routine, the deadening reiteration of everything, keep us at a distance from Him. We need to recover ourselves, and with quiet leisure to take our seat in the path of His goings until He pass by. How often in the year is there a chance for meditation? Nay, how many of us remember even what the word means?

Thought we know, and speech; still better do we know action. Prayer we know, and reading and worship; but what is this Eastern notion to which the Bible refers? To meditate one must be still, fenced off for a prescribed time from the pressure of duties, indifferent to pleasure, free from pain. Then one must propose to the imagination not books or men, or even nature, but simply God— God in the circle of the heavens, God in the swaying movements of the waters, God in the secret places of the earth; above all, God in the soul. And then one must wait and believe, for the rest is with Him; avenues open, and from vistas hands beckon, silences become vocal, and the throb of the Life of the Universe is perceived at its heart. Personal being dies in the consciousness of a Personal Being which is not you, but in which you are. You are in contact with Truth. That is the soul-refreshing goal of every holiday.

Dawn.

Some say that ever 'gainst that season comes
Wherein our Saviour's birth is celebrated,
The bird of dawning singeth all night long . . .
So hallow'd and so gracious is the time.
                       HAMLET, *Act* 1, *Scene* 1.

THAT was a quaint fancy. On Christmas eve the cock crowed through the night. Truths, once wrapped in fables, often prove to be true when they are discovered to be fabulous. And though it be certain that the cock does not change his habit for the auspicious day, yet is it true as truth itself that the Incarnation was as it were the Dawn of the World, and its celebration should yearly turn upon that rapturous morning-joy. What went before it belonged to the watches of the night. The ancient religions, the Western philosophies, the long Jewish preparation, were songs before sunrise.

There's a budding morrow in midnight.

Plato and Isaiah, Virgil and John Baptist, were voices of that morrow which was coming. Christ was the morrow itself, not budding, but a-bloom. The heralds of the dawn called across the mountains, and then the morning strode from ridge to ridge towards a perfect day.

There is, therefore, a profound and lovely truth in the idea that on the coming of Christmas the bird of dawning does not slumber and wake, but utters his shrill cry from sunset to sunrise.

Old mythologies told in a thousand beautiful tales the recurrent fact of dawn. The best known, perhaps the most beautiful, is that of Aurora, who comes from the East in a chariot convoyed by the Hours, and drawn by steeds that trample the darkness into rosy flames. But our Dawn, instead of giving to the phenomena of Nature the lively traits and colours of personality, fetches all the analogies and parables of Nature to illustrate the supreme Personal Event. The myths were guesses at truth. The Truth is the answer to the queries. All the tales of the wonders of the Dawn are gathered together, completed and interpreted, in the coming of Christ. That was the true Light that lighteth every man coming into the world. That was the Sun of Righteousness that rises with healing on His wings.

It was well-feigned, therefore,

that all through that blissful night the cock heralded the Dawn.

Now for a long time we have found more pleasure in the secondary associations of Christmas than in the fact which gave to Christmas both name and meaning. Confess it, you are more interested in your cards and presents than in the song the Angels sang. Those social gatherings, with the hearty laughter of family friends, and the good cheer following on the skating or the riding or the dancing, the sparkle of frost, the shrouded white of winter landscape and the glow of ruddy sunsets, the yule log on the hearth, and the berries on the walls, some suggestions of old times, of our grandfathers and their grandfathers keeping Christmas, the story, the jest, the pensive reminiscence, the sense of gathering years and the mirth of children, these touch the chords of Christmas more tripplingly than the great world-arching truth of the Son of God made flesh. The mummers in the night and the quaint customs of a near antiquity are more akin to us than the choirs of admiring angels and the deeds which were done "from the foundation of the world."

But I would make the somewhat startling assertion that of all the interests and delights of Christmas the central one is the most thrilling and absorbing. Let those, therefore, on whom the modern Christmas has begun to pall, to whom Christmas morning breaks heavily with a sound of vanished joys and the vacancies of loss, strike backward to the great event which made the Dawn of the world, the Incarnation of the Son of God.

I need not remind you that on that first Christmas night the whole world lay rocked in a monotonous despair. There was no assurance of progress; there were many signs of decline; the myths said that the Golden Age had been, and through silver, iron and clay, was sinking down into a final ruin. Suddenly came the Dawn, and the Golden Age was a-head for hearts to yearn after and lives to strive for. The secular religions were crystallisations of despair. The religion of the Manger was a flowing fountain of Hope. "Forward" was the cry which rang along the world. "The best is yet to be" became the song of poets. And men lifted up their eyes to a heavenly city descending out of heaven, attired as a bride.

Crow, happy bird, through the dark watches; the dawn is at hand.

That was a gay portrait of a beloved woman which described, though eyes were like stars and hair like twilight,

> All things else about her drawn
> From Maytime and the cheerful dawn.

It was a fair description of the new bride-look in the earth. If there were eyes which still held in their depths the sorrow of a vanquished sin; if there was a mantle of the shadow of death over beings who must through death enter into life, the new note struck was all of the jocund light and of the growing day.

And as each Christmas is added to the tale there is a record, widening especially in these latter years, of the dawn reaching new regions of those who sit in darkness and the shadow of death. This light silvers the Eastern pines on new mountain-ranges year by year. It has struck the line of those islands far withdrawn in the waste seas of the East, Japan, and Southward, the rude uplands of New Guinea. A shout has run along the isles inhabited by the most civilised and the most savage, of heathen peoples, "The Dawn, the Dawn." It has fallen full and flaming on Uganda, where the fountains of the Day are opened, and distant African tribes begin to feel the shock of a nation at the heart of the Dark Continent born in a day. Still round the world circles the buoyant clarion of the day. And where last Christmas there was darkness, this Christmas there is light. The hallowed and gracious time is intelligible where "Peace on earth and goodwill to men" had not been even a dream. " Be of good

cheer, I have overcome the world."
It is good hearing, and we can
confidently wait for the ingathering of the trophies. Who would
grow impatient when the flush of
the light has struck the Western
mountains, because in front the
sun climbs slow—how slowly!

Look Westward, all the land is light.

It is a high and spirit-moving
assurance. The giants of darkness are veritably chased and
smitten hip and thigh by the ad-
vancing warriors of the light. Let
the bird of dawning sing all night
long!

Joseph Rabinovitch, the Russian
Jew, trained in the Hebrew Scrip-
tures and the Talmud, and at the
age of forty brought to the revelation of the Son of God, says: "I
was like a man living in a house
furnished with every article of

furniture which money could buy, and yet the shutters of that house were closed and the curtains all drawn, so that I was in the dark, and knew not the meaning of my own learning till Jesus, the Light of the world came in, and illumined all as in a flash." So it was with the world in the first century, so it is with the world before Christ comes, still. So it was with that learned Rabbinist, Paul. So it is with the Russian Jew, Rabinovitch. There is darkness and perplexity; the meaning of things is not perceived; all ordered knowledge lacks its source, its motive, its end; until the cry of dawn and the light streaming in, which is Jesus.

"Back to Christ" is a favourite cry of Theology to-day. "Christ back to us" is the new cry of Religion. This Christmas is surely of all the eighteen hundred and ninety-six the most luminous with His coming, the most jubilant in His arrival. Look not for the streaks of the morning in the dark heavens of the political world; nor listen for the glad cock-crow in the purlieus of fashion and pleasure, where, as of old, the sounds of revelry drown the significant and eternal voices. But consider the streaks of the Dawn, and listen to the herald of its coming, in the widening work of Missions, in the Church's yearning for union, in the tender desire to alleviate distress, and in the growing expectation of social reform. It is hard, impossible, to be pessimistic, or to doubt that He who shall come will come, and is, indeed, coming with the clouds of Heaven.

"So hallowed and so gracious is

the time." I omitted at the head of this essay the words which tell that on this Christmas night evil spirits and the conjurations of witchcraft might not walk the earth. Indeed, it is that flush of the coming of Christ into the heart and the life which chases the gloomy influences of the nether-world and the gloomy superstitions which made the old world sad. When His coming is ignored or unperceived, how rapidly the old haunting horrors and "damned ghosts" of the earth revive! Mark the literature of His absence, the books, novels, poems, &c., which in these latter years come from those modern men of the City of Dreadful Night, who have lost the Dawn-spirit, Christ. God has a great argument for His Light—His Incarnate Son—His holy way of saving men; it is this that where it is not, shadows fall, and where it is rejected the blackest and most haunted night usurps the spirit of man. There are parts of the world where the night is that which precedes the dawn, hopeful, promising, expectant. There are also parts where the night is the triple darkness of a dawn stamped out and defied.

But this we may put from us for awhile, and cherish the kindly faith, nursed by the fervent prayer, that we and ours may be humble recipients of the light, and numbered among Christ's Children of the Day.

R. L. Stevenson's Christmas Sermon.

FAR away in the West, the centre of a crowded square in the Chinese quarter of San Francisco, is the fountain which the zeal of Americans has reared to the memory of that dauntless Bayard of literature, Robert Louis Stevenson. Stevenson passed through San Francisco, and to have passed through a place was enough to leave a trail of his indefinable charm, and to have raised up some hearts that loved him. And this fountain, the work of a rising sculptor, who was captivated by the romantic story of Stevenson's death and burial, now stands as a witness in the Golden Gate of the West, where the impetuous West is brought up sharp by the East which it has overtaken, that Stevenson more than any modern writer has an indefeasible claim to the hearts of the East and of the West, of the North from which he came, of the South where he went to die.

With rare discrimination the sculptor has selected as the inscription on the fountain a sentence from Stevenson's *Christmas Sermon*, the text of it, one might almost say. Henceforth, the people who throng that cosmopolitan city, if, at least, they have learnt the English tongue, will in quenching their thirst see looking into their eyes a soul that utters these brave words:

"*To be honest, to be kind, to earn a little and to spend a little less; to make upon the whole a family happier by his presence; to renounce where that shall be necessary, and not to be embittered; to keep a few friends, but these without capitulation; above all, on the same grim conditions, to keep friends with himself; here is a task for all that a man has of fortitude and delicacy."*

And if the drinker at the fountain inquires who spoke these brave words, let us hope the answer will be: "One who made them a reality." He may not read the books, written with such heroic resolution in the respites of illness. Indeed, the subjects of Stevenson's books can hardly claim to be of the immortal order, and it is not, perhaps, possible to live, except as a memory, on the mere strength of style. But this sentence, this text of a Christmas sermon, will be read, and no reader but will be the better for it, as long as the fountain stands.

To say that it contains the whole duty of man would be extravagant. It has not, it must be owned, a theological ring; and for anything that appears, one might hold its doctrines without being religious at all. But to practise these doctrines, to live in the spirit of this creed, certainly implies a great grasp of the essence of religion, and must be the fruit of a very fine theology. Is it conceivable that a wise and righteous God could regard with anything but affection one who had lived in the practice of these homely virtues? Here is the off-hand description of one whom every one is bound to love. Can God, who is love, condemn one whom every one is bound to love?

It is at Christmas-time that a

creed of this kind commends itself and makes a bid to be accepted as the guiding principle of the year. And if it has not too much the air of a sermon, *not* of the Stevenson kind, a sermon such as we preach in pulpits, I shall beg leave to examine the clauses one by one.

"*To be honest.*" It is worth observing that the stronger your religious principles are, the more constraint has to be laid upon you by yourself, to be honest. For if it once comes to be the main object of life to make a proselyte, it will require an unusual grace not to think that all means are permissible in securing him. It is a tribute to the intensity of the Jesuit's convictions that Jesuitism has become another word for dishonesty. It is probably for this reason that in our weaker moments we prefer people of weak or no convictions to zealots for a faith. The former, we find, are more honest. The latter are always compassing sea and land to make a proselyte. One can hardly love a man whose object is to chase Dissent out of his parish, because he would have to be an angel to avoid dishonest ways of doing it; and if he were an angel he would not be anxious to get rid of Dissent. "Here is a task, then, for all that a man has of fortitude and delicacy"—merely to be honest.

"*To be kind.*" That is not by any means easy. At Christmas time we enjoy a favourable spasm of kindness. But that is a species of intoxication. "When he gets drunk," I read of the Russian moujik, "which is whenever beneficent chance affords, he leans for hours against a fence or wall, smiling gently at the passers-by. If he makes any demonstration, it is to throw his arms round some other moujik's neck and kiss him. The drunker he is the more affectionately fraternal he becomes." In the semi-inebriety of Christmas festivities there is a great deal which passes for kindness in persons essentially unkind. But to be kind all the year round, and to all—to be kind, for example, to those whom it is your duty to rebuke, and to be kind when your nerves are fretted by pain and overwork—that makes a considerable demand upon you. It is a temper of mind which you will hardly hit, except by a strong religious principle. And if kindness be taken in anything like an absolute sense, you may be challenged to show an instance of it in one who is not a Christian. A charity "which suffers long and is kind" is a stream drawn from only one perennial fountain. That Stevenson himself was, in his later years, uniformly kind to Samoan or to European, to troublesome visitors and to the home circle, we have abundant evidence. I should venture to infer from that fact alone that he was a Christian. I have known, on the other hand, some people who pass as Christians guilty of almost incredible acts of unkindness, which suggest that all the vital sap of charity has been used up in a few directions, leaving the best part of the system dry.

"*To earn a little and spend a little less.*" 'Tis an admirable trait. Frankly, are there any people in this world more intolerable than the beggars who never earn, but live by sponging on the benevolent, unless they be those persons who do their share in earning but always overstep their income, and fall back on more careful friends to meet their deficits? I grant that generosity is a fine virtue, and the world offers fine opportunities of exercising it. But the whine of the impecunious, and the bland childishness of the spendthrift, do not train the virtue of generosity. We give to them with the awful qualm that we are probably feeding the flame that is destroying them; we fling our money at them to be rid of them, and know in our hearts that we have won their hatred because we have not given enough. On the whole, I like no trait of character better than that which makes your generous Scot " earn a little and spend less."

" To make upon the whole a family

happier by his presence." Oh! the delicate modesty of that "upon the whole." And oh! the exquisite spirit that conceives this among the primary and essential virtues, "to make a family happier by his presence." I imagine that hell is a place, not in itself uncomfortable or insalubrious, but entirely inhabited by those who have *not* made a family happier by their presence, and now those who *have* are withdrawn, and these are left to themselves, a big household of the morose, the selfish, the unsocial, reaping their appropriate reward.

"*To renounce—and not to be embittered.*" This cuts down into the quick of life. Renunciation is so inevitable in this world—that is, it is forced upon you by such stress of circumstance, that to renounce in itself is no better a virtue than to freeze in winter cold, or at the end of life to die. But in the renunciations which are not to be avoided, to retain the sweetness of those who do not renounce; to give up the joy and never to refer to it; to seriously believe that in the lopping and the pruning, in the pinch of heart, and the desolation, and the chill, lies precisely the best for you and for all—this is infinitely loveable, it distils the fine dews and fragrance of the soul.

"*To keep a few friends, but these without capitulation.*" Certainly, for an ill-world lays siege to our friendships, and ceases not day or night to demand their surrender. If you will have friends you do not fight for, or starve for, or suffer for, you will have none. Nay, they are scarcely friends in the true and tried sense until you have refused capitulation for them, and chosen death for yourself rather. It is a good test of a man to find how many of his friends are those whom he has had for years. One who has alienated many friends, and counts many foes that once were friends, reveals to you his own character in recounting their perfidy.

And "*to keep friends with himself*" without capitulation. That is not the slightest task of the man who would be beloved, nor does it make the least severe demands upon his fortitude and delicacy. Stevenson is not talking of self-complacency, but of that which is the secret of dignity and of sweetness, the frank admission to yourself that you are an imperfect fellow upon whom you must not be too hard, the cheerfulness which does not tolerate self-disgust, the charity so wide that it at last returns to be charitable even to you.

Christmas is a good time for drinking at this fountain near the Western Gate, and for lifting up our eyes to this imperishable legend.

www.ingramcontent.com/pod-product-compliance
Lightning Source LLC
Chambersburg PA
CBHW020106170426
43199CB00009B/422